Dingle Way

Slí Chorca Dhuibhne

Sandra Bardwell
and
Jacquetta Megarry

Rucksack Readers

Dingle Way

Third edition, fully revised, published in 2019

Rucksack Readers, 6 Old Church Lane, Edinburgh, EH15 3PX, UK

Telephone 0131 661 0262

Website   *www.rucsacs.com*

Email   **info@rucsacs.com**

Distributed in North America by Interlink Publishing, 46 Crosby Street, Northampton, Mass., 01060, USA (*www.interlinkbooks.com*)

ISBN 978-1-898481-89-8

British Library cataloguing in publication data: a catalogue record for this book is available from the British Library.

Designed in Scotland by Ian Clydesdale (*www.workhorse.scot*)

The mapping in this book was created by Lovell Johns with data from *OpenStreetMap.org* © OpenStreetMap contributors, CC-by-SA, combined with updates from original fieldwork by the authors.

Printed in the UK by Blackmore Ltd on rainproof, biodegradable paper.

Publisher's note

All information was checked prior to publication. However, changes are inevitable: take local advice and look out for waymarkers and other signage e.g. for diversions. Walkers are advised to check two websites for updates before setting out: *www.dingleway.com* and *www.rucsacs.com/books/dgw*.

Parts of the Way are wet underfoot, others are remote, and the weather is unpredictable year-round. Crossing streams requires great care, especially when in spate, and one part of the Way may not be safely passable in mist or low cloud. You are responsible for your own safety, for ensuring that your clothing, food and equipment are suited to your needs and that your intended walk can be safely completed in daylight. The publisher cannot accept any liability for any ill-health, injury or loss arising directly or indirectly from reading this book.

Feedback is welcome and will be rewarded

All feedback will be followed up, and readers whose comments lead to changes are entitled to claim a free copy of our next edition upon publication. Please email your comments to *info@rucsacs.com*.

Contents

Introduction

The Dingle Way can claim perhaps the finest scenery and richest archaeological heritage of all Ireland's 32 Waymarked Ways. Throughout its 183 km (114 miles) it combines wild coasts and cliff-tops with superb uplands and beautiful, tranquil and fertile countryside.

Starting and finishing in Tralee, County Kerry's largest town, the route resembles the outline of a leaf on a stalk. The stalk comprises the first, and most of the last, day's walking. It supports the leaf, which encircles the Dingle Peninsula, seldom far from the coast, passing close to Europe's most westerly point. Through small villages and farmlands, over moorlands, and along coastal cliffs and vast beaches, the Dingle Way is magnificently scenic, providing ever-changing vistas that linger in your memory.

Highlights include the wild moorland on the lower slopes of the Slieve Mish mountains, overlooking Tralee Bay; the beautiful white ribbon of Inch Strand; charming Annascaul village in its wide, fertile valley, overlooked by the mountains; the picturesque town of Dingle, set in its sheltered harbour; the superb traverse of the lower slopes of Mount Eagle strewn with archaeological features; the glorious, rugged coastline seen from the cliff-tops north of Clogher; the traverse of the northern shoulder of Brandon Mountain, and the exhilarating freedom of the extended beach walk right around the shores of the Maharees Peninsula, between Brandon and Tralee Bays. Wherever you go, you'll find friendly, welcoming people, ready to dispense their uniquely Irish brand of hospitality.

Looking north-west towards Sybil Point, and the island An Fiach

Planning to walk the Way

The Way makes use of a variety of routes throughout its length. Several beaches provide glorious walking along wide sands, mainly on the north coast between Cloghane and Lower Camp (about 17% of the Way). It also uses historic paths such as the line of the old Tralee to Dingle road, boreens, farm tracks and paths round field edges or cliff tops.

However, in common with other Irish Ways, this one involves a considerable distance of road-walking, much more than visitors might expect. Overall, about 48% of it follows tarmac (bitumen) roads, though nearly half of this is over once you reach Dingle at the end of the third day. This partly reflects the fact that Irish communities were (and to some extent still are) widely separated, and that, in the past, people moved about on foot or by donkey. It also reveals that rights of way are almost non-existent in Ireland, and that it is difficult to secure access to land off-road.

Fortunately the road walking is very varied, almost always scenic and is mostly along quiet lanes with very little traffic. However, remember that large tractors are frequent road users, that there are many blind bends and that most minor roads are narrow and lined with high hedges. If two vehicles need to pass each other, retreat to the verge – if there is one – and wait until the road is clear.

North-east from Smerwick Harbour towards Ballydavid Head

Restaurant in Castlegregory

An attractive feature of the Way is how it passes through so many villages where you can find accommodation, pubs, places to eat, and usually also a shop. This means you don't have to allow for any significant walking distance on top of the overall total merely to reach (or return from) your destination or overnight stay.

Elevation, pace and waymarking

The Way is generally a low-level walk, with only one significant ascent – in the north-west, up and over a spur of Brandon Mountain at 650 m. Elsewhere the route never rises above 230 m, although there are plenty of minor ups and downs as you cross small valleys or headlands. Depending on the season and recent weather, several sections may be boggy, some extremely so: this applies to most boreens and farm tracks, parts of the moorland path between Blennerville and Camp, to the offroad section east of Feohanagh and to the steep descent from Mount Brandon.

Conditions underfoot will reduce your average speed, as will the number of people if you walk in a group. Groups travel at the pace of their slowest member, or a little less. Overall, expect to average 3-4 km/hr, (2-2½ mph) unless you're particularly fit and impatient to press on.

The route is waymarked, mainly with black posts bearing a distinctive yellow walker icon and an arrow head, plus some fingerposts. However, you still need to watch where you're going: it's easy to overshoot a turning, perhaps because a crucial waymarker has been used as a rubbing-post by animals, removed by souvenir hunters or even vandalised. At some junctions, you need to notice paint splashed on a rock, arrows on poles or other subtle clues.

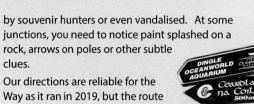

Our directions are reliable for the Way as it ran in 2019, but the route has changed over the years, and may change further. Superseded waymarkers are sometimes left in place, which can be confusing. Rely on your own common sense and map reading, and remain vigilant.

It's vital to detect a mistake quickly. If you haven't seen a waymarker for 20 minutes or so, or if you reach a completely unmarked junction, question whether you are still on the Way (albeit markers on beaches are normally sparse). If in doubt, retrace your steps and check your position from the map and directions.

The brand 'Kerry Camino' was launched in 2012 and its website claims this name for the first three sections of Dingle Way (from Tralee to Dingle). To download a logbook and locate stamping stations (mainly in pubs and shops) visit *www.kerrycamino.com*. Much of the route is part of the 'Wild Atlantic Way' which covers all 2500 km (1550 miles) of Ireland's Atlantic coastline. You will see its blue logo with white waves on many road signs.

Waymarking on Brandon Mountain

Crossing a stream on Fermoyle Strand

Beach walking, tides and stream crossing

The long stretches of beach walking are a major feature of the Way, and most of Dingle's beaches can be walked safely at nearly all states of the tide. If you are unlucky enough to face stormy weather, be cautious of walking on a beach around high water, especially during 'spring tides' of up to four or five metres. 'Springs' have nothing to do with seasons: they are very high tides that occur for a few days, twice per lunar month, about or just after the new and full moon. It may then be safer to take to the dunes, or to bypass the beach using roads. Remember that the flatter the beach, the faster the tide will seem to come in.

High water occurs twice per lunar day (roughly 25 hours), but local landforms and weather can vary both timing and height of the tide. Tide tables are available locally for a couple of euros. If relying on them be sure to allow for local variation (Dingle high water is up to an hour ahead of the times printed for Cobh, near Cork) and for summer time: when in force, this may be an hour ahead of the time shown in tide tables.

Normally, the state of the tide affects walkers more in relation to whether the vast expanses of sand are visible, how firm the sand is to walk on, and where and how you choose to cross the various streams. In warm weather you may choose to walk barefoot anyway, but in colder weather you may need to take off your boots to keep them dry when crossing the occasional stream.

Safety and weather

The Dingle Way deserves to be taken seriously – it passes close to precipitous cliff edges, crosses exposed moorland, and traverses tidal shores. Even a minor accident can have major consequences, though for most of the Way help should never be very far away. It's safer to walk in a group, but if you decide to go solo, think how you would handle an emergency, remembering that mobile phone coverage is patchy, and that a dead battery makes a mobile useless.

The weather has a crucial bearing on your plans: check the forecast daily before setting out; check *www.met.ie* or ask locally. Rain is always likely, and the weather is unpredictable and very changeable year-round. It's vital to have the right gear: without effective waterproofs, the risk of becoming chilled or hypothermic is high. Damp feet can cause serious blisters which could ruin (or even curtail) your holiday.

New to long distance walking?

If you haven't done much walking before, it is advisable to tackle the Way with someone who knows how to use a map and compass. Note that our mapping has a km grid and also shows distances in km for a clockwise circuit from Tralee to Camp.

Well before you leave for Dingle, do a few day walks (at least four hours long) to test your footwear and to build up fitness. Comfortable, waterproof boots are the first essential. For advice on choosing gear, obtain our *Notes for Novices*: see page 71.

Clockwise or anticlockwise?

Most people walk the Way clockwise, turning south from near Camp village towards the south coast of the peninsula. That way, you will be well into your stride before you face the toughest ascent and longest days.

How long will it take?

The full distance of 183 km (114 miles) is commonly regarded as an eight-day walk, though it can be done in less by combining sections to make very long days, or by using public transport to bypass certain sections. You may prefer to spend more than eight days, for example to allow for a visit to Great Blasket Island (see page 28), or to take in other side trips.

Fortunately, little extra time needs to be allowed to reach places with accommodation. If you choose somewhere more than 1-2 km from the Way, ask in advance whether your host can provide a lift. If so, it's customary to make a small cash payment to cover fuel. The drawback is that you need to make a firm commitment to a pick-up time and place at the end of the day. Phone to confirm arrival at the rendezvous – assuming that you have a signal on your mobile (cellphone).

Some walkers save time by using a bus to start and/or finish at Camp instead of Tralee. Others take a bus to start from Dingle and/or return to Tralee by bus from Camp (or on a Friday from Cloghane or Castlegregory). Study the website *www.buseirann.ie* carefully. Don't underestimate the time you need to appreciate the scenery and wildlife, and perhaps to make side-trips. Enjoy your walk to the utmost.

If there's a driver in your group, it's easy to arrange pick-ups: each day's walk ends in a town or village. Please park considerately, preferably in a formal car park. Leaving cars in passing places or in front of gates may infuriate someone and is often dangerous.

Daily distances
(rounded) for an 8-day itinerary

	km	mi
Tralee		
	18·4	11·4
Camp		
	15·7	9·8
Annascaul		
	22·5	14·0
Dingle		
	22·4	13·9
Dunquin		
	23·1	14·4
Feohanagh		
	25·7	16·0
Cloghane		
	26·4	16·4
Castlegregory		
	10·4	6·8
Camp		
	18·4	11·4
Tralee		
Total (rounded)	183	114

Bus services *Check www.buseirann.ie before relying on these buses*

Travel planning

Many visitors to Ireland will arrive at Dublin by air or by ferry: see page 71. Dublin has a good train service to Tralee: Irish Rail plies between Dublin Heuston and Tralee stations, with about six services daily, mostly with a change at Mallow, and an average journey time of about 4 hours. Aer Lingus operates flights between Dublin (and other airports) to Kerry: see below.

Bus Éireann operates frequent daily services between Dublin bus station (Busaras) and Tralee, with a change at Limerick or Cork, and a journey time of about 7 hours.

See p71 for transport information

Ryanair offers direct flights to Kerry airport (at Farranfore) from London (Stansted or Luton) and from two German airports (Frankfurt Hahn and Berlin Schönefeld). Buses link the airport with Tralee.

By road the distance from Dublin is about 300 km (190 miles); roads are generally good as far as Limerick, less so beyond. Journeys may take longer than you expect: the main road passes through many small towns where traffic congestion is an issue.

What is the best time of year?

Except perhaps for mid-winter, the Way can be walked in any month. Be prepared for cold, wet and windy conditions at any time, and you may be pleasantly surprised. Think about these issues before deciding:

- Winter days are short: at Dingle's latitude (52° N), there are only 7-8 hours of daylight in December, leaving little or no margin for error on most days.
- In winter, public transport may be less frequent, or non-existent.
- Many B&Bs close for the winter, and certain side-trips (notably, Great Blasket) are not available: see page 28.
- Midges and horse-flies can be very annoying in summer.
- During the busy tourist season (July/August), accommodation may be difficult to find without advance booking.
- All in all, the ideal months are May/June and September/October.

Responsible walking

The countryside provides its residents' livelihood; it is their workplace and your playground, where common sense and courtesy are the rules of the game and the basis of the widely accepted 'Code of Conduct' (see panel). The Occupiers' Liability Act 1995 puts an obligation on all who enter a farm to do everything necessary to ensure their own safety and to accept responsibility for any damage to private property, livestock and crops resulting from their actions. Pass through farms unobtrusively and keep well clear of livestock, crops, machinery and farming activities. Your presence can cause stress to animals and jeopardise your own safety. Give a wide berth to cattle, especially those with calves, pregnant ewes, young lambs, and ewes with lambs.

Remember that it's a privilege to walk through someone else's property – follow the Code to the letter.

> ### Walkers' Code of Conduct
> ✓ Leave all farm gates as you find them
> ✓ Keep to the waymarked route
> ✓ Always use gates and stiles; avoid climbing fences, hedges and walls
> ✓ Take all your litter home
> ✓ Guard against all risk of fire
> ✓ Go carefully on country roads
> ✓ Help keep water supplies pure
> ✓ Protect wildlife, plants and trees
> ✓ Take heed of warning signs
> ✓ Immediately report any damage caused by your actions to the farmer or landowner
> ✓ Keep children under close supervision at all times
> ✓ Go quietly – avoid unnecessary noise
> ✓ Large groups are intrusive – keep numbers low

Dogs

You may meet locals walking their dogs along parts of the Way, but the official advice is: 'Do not bring dogs on any section of the Way which crosses farmland. The Way often crosses fields grazed by cattle and sheep, and any dog seen chasing domestic animals is quite likely to be shot.' Access is a fraught issue between walkers and landowners. Our advice is to avoid needless conflict and difficulties with accommodation and refreshments by leaving your dog at home.

Looking west along Fermoyle Strand

Accommodation

	B&B/hotel	hostel	pub/café
Tralee	✓	✓	✓
Camp	✓	✓	✓
Inch	✓	✓	✓
Annascaul	✓	✓	✓
Dingle	✓	✓	✓
Ventry	✓	✓	✓
Dunquin	✓	✓	✓
Ballyferriter	✓		✓
Feohanagh	✓		✓
Ballydavid	✓	✓	✓
Cuas	✓		✓
Cloghane	✓	✓	
Castlegregory	✓		✓

The Dingle Way is blessed with a variety of accessible accommodation to suit all tastes and budgets. Whatever your choice, it's wise to book ahead to ensure that you don't have to compromise your preferences or your bank balance. Official websites or publications are the best sources of information; alternatively, sign up with a tour operator whose programme features the Way.

Many B&Bs and guest houses are registered with Fáilte Ireland (Ireland's Tourism Development Authority) and can be booked through the local tourist authority's website. Such accommodation ensures high standards – a comfortable bed and almost always private bathroom facilities, plus a substantial cooked breakfast. However, some good B&Bs choose not to pay the Board's affiliation fee; standards can vary but many offer great value. These unregistered places may seem more difficult to contact for advance booking, but web searching will bring results.

To keep costs down, consider staying at hostels. There were hostels in nine places along the Way in 2019: see the table above and page 70 for contact details, but hostels open and close from time to time, so check well in advance. Standards vary, but in an intensely competitive market, shoddy operators don't survive for long. Expect a bed in a dormitory or a private room, possibly with private bathroom, and use of a communal kitchen.

The cheapest accommodation is carried on your back. If you're happy to carry a tent, sleeping bag, food and cooking equipment, and to cope with bad weather, you can be completely independent. In season, there are commercial campsites with a range of facilities in Tralee, Dingle, Castlegregory and near Camp. All Irish land is privately owned and you should ask permission to camp on enclosed (fenced) ground; elsewhere, camp

Camping Code

- ✓ All Irish land is privately owned; ask permission before camping in an enclosed field
- ✓ Camp out of sight of roads, houses and popular areas
- ✓ Move on after one night
- ✓ Use stoves, not open fires
- ✓ Help to keep water supplies pure
- ✓ Bury human waste completely, at least 30m away from paths or streams
- ✓ Remove all other litter
- ✓ Leave your pitch as you found it, or better
- ✓ Keep groups small.

discreetly. You'll also need to purify water, given the presence of sheep everywhere. Follow the widely accepted Camping Code.

Irish placenames and Dingle town

The Dingle peninsula is part of the Gaeltacht and preserving the Irish language is a cultural priority of the government: see page 19. The Irish versions of placenames look unfamiliar to most visitors, but they are arguably more authentic than the anglicised versions. The further west you go, the less likely you are to see English placenames. The OSi Discovery maps no longer show any English names in the Gaeltacht. For clarity, and without disrespect for the Irish language, our mapping shows English names. Our text also

English	pronounced	*Irish*
Tralee		*Trá Lí*
Camp		*An Com*
Annascaul	anna skole	*Abhainn an Scáil*
Dingle		*Daingean Uí Chúis*
Ventry		*Ceann Trá*
Dunquin		*Dún Chaoin*
Feohanagh	fee och nah	*An Fheothanach*
Ballycurrane		*Baile ui Chorráin*
Brandon		*Cé Chréanainn*
Cloghane	cla haan	*An Clochán*
Castlegregory		*Caisleán Ghriaire*
Great Blasket		*An Blascaod Mór*

gives the Gaelic version when space permits. This table shows the main villages in the order you will encounter them on your walk; see also the alphabetic list on our inside back cover.

The name for Dingle town has been hotly debated ever since the Irish government tried to proscribe the world-recognised name Dingle in 2005. The citizens of Dingle were outraged, and in 2011 another law created a bilingual compromise. What you see on the ground may depend on the age of the sign. For more, see *www.dinglename.com*.

What to bring

The greatest freedom comes through being totally self-sufficient and carrying everything on your back: to do this, you need to be experienced and fit. Staying overnight in a B&B or hostel means a much lighter load. If you use the services of a tour operator, this should include baggage transfer: see page 62.

Once on the Way, make sure you set out each day with plenty of food and drink. There are shops at the beginning and end of each of the recommended stages; alternatively, some accommodation hosts will, with sufficient notice, provide a packed lunch. It's not a good idea to depend on finding shops or pubs open during each day's walk because opening days and hours vary widely.

If you need to phone accommodation hosts, remember that public phones are scarce. If you are relying on a mobile phone, monitor the signal level while on high ground, in case the signal disappears when you lose altitude.

Packing checklist

We list essential items first, then desirable ones – obviously a matter of opinion, but still a useful starting-point. If you haven't walked in Ireland before, consider two points: first, gaiters are invaluable, whether ankle gaiters or knee-high, ideally the wraparound kind that are easy to fit. Second, if you haven't worn your waterproof trousers recently, test them before you go, while there's still time to re-proof or replace them.

Essential

- rucksack large enough to carry all items, with space to spare (e.g. 35 litres)
- comfortable, waterproof walking boots
- gaiters to keep mud and water out of boots and off trouser legs
- suitable clothing, including specialist walking socks
- waterproof jacket and over-trousers
- hat (for warmth and/or sun protection) and gloves
- dry clothes and footwear to change into
- waterproof rucksack cover or liner(s), e.g. garbage or garden refuse bag
- guidebook, map and compass
- enough food to last between supply points
- first aid kit, including blister treatment
- insect repellent for midges and/or horse flies in summer, especially on calm days
- toilet tissue (preferably biodegradable)
- personal toiletries, including towel if hostelling
- enough cash in euros. There are cash machines in Tralee, Camp and Dingle; credit cards are widely but not universally accepted.

Desirable

- walking poles
- whistle and torch: essential if you are walking alone or in winter
- spare socks and small towel (for stream crossings)
- sun and wind protection for skin and eyes
- binoculars – useful for watching wildlife
- camera (ideally light and robust) plus spare batteries, memory cards or film
- notebook and pen
- mobile phone (but only if you can conserve its battery level).
- If you are camping, add to the above list a tent, sleeping gear, food, cooking utensils, a portable stove and fuel – and a much larger rucksack to carry it all.

2·1 Archaeology

The Dingle peninsula has a rich archaeological heritage with many remarkably well-preserved features. It is thought that people arrived here from Spain and western France at least 4000 years ago; they cultivated the ground and buried their dead in massive graves. Celtic peoples reached Ireland around 300 BC and, among much else, built forts, many of which have survived. Christianity arrived in about AD 400 with St Patrick and was spread by his numerous followers; many archaeological features reflect religious beliefs and practices.

The following paragraphs outline the main types of these features you'll see along or near the Way, described in chronological order.

Standing stones and stone circles

These are among the oldest features in the area, dating at least from the Bronze Age (from 2000 BC) and are thought to have been built for ritual purposes. They are marked on OSi maps by various words including *clocháin*, *cloiche* and *cloch*.

Isolated tall stones (*gallán*, *dallán* or *líagán*) stand up to 5 m high, and may also have signified burial sites. Some bear carved or incised early Christian crosses and are known as carved stones, cross-inscribed stones or cross slabs.

A stone circle is a ring about 15 m in diameter, consisting of vertical stones up to 1·5 m tall. However, it is rare to find complete circles standing intact.

Dolmens

Called *tuama meigiliteach* in Irish, dolmens are megalithic tombs (i.e. graves made of big stones) probably dating from after 2000 BC. The name dolmen comes from the Breton words for 'stone table'. They usually comprise up to seven upright stones forming a rectangular chamber, narrower at one end, and with one or two slabs for the roof.

Cathair Deargain fortified homesteads

Ogham

Perhaps the most enigmatic and mysterious of all Irish archaeological features, Ogham is an ancient alphabet consisting of dashes or short straight lines, usually cut along one or more edges of a flat stone. Twenty letters have been identified, constituting the earliest inscriptions in the Irish language. The carvings apparently represent people's names, suggesting that the stones may have served as memorials. The earliest examples were carved in about AD 500, and Ogham continued to be used, though not widely, for centuries. There's a very fine example at the highest point of the Way, at the col on Brandon Mountain: see page 59. The notches may be translated as 'Ronan the priest, son of Comgan'.

Notches along the right edge represent Ogham characters

Promontory forts

Often sited in amazingly precarious locations along the coast, these defensive structures used natural features, perhaps to protect tribal lands. A deep wide ditch was dug, or a massive stone wall built across the narrowest part of a promontory cutting off its seaward end. Another ditch on the landward side sometimes gave extra protection. Promontory forts generally date from the Iron Age (about 300 BC to AD 500). Dún an Óir is a splendid example: see page 53.

Ring-forts

Ring-forts date from the early Christian era, and are quite common, although their names vary: lios, dún, rath, caher, cashel or fort. They are usually circular or D-shaped enclosures between 25 and 50 m across, with an earth-and-stone wall. In some cases this is surrounded by a further massive wall, or a ditch and bank. The interior usually appears empty, though originally it would have contained timber or stone dwellings. Some forts may have been built for defence, but most were probably built to enclose a family group's house and associated buildings.

Enclosures

Within the modern pattern of rectangular fields, the sites of former stone-walled enclosures are sometimes visible as circular or irregular shaped outlines. These usually enclosed an entire community, large or small. Since the structures were normally wooden, the traces most likely to be seen today are the low, grassy mounds of grave headstones or the rectangular outline of a stone-built chapel. They may be indicated on maps by the term killeen (*ceallúnach* in Irish) meaning children's graveyards – the resting places of unbaptised children.

Clocháns

These small round buildings, known as 'beehive' huts, are superb examples of the skilful use of stone. Built of circular layers, each with a slightly smaller diameter than the one below, they are topped (or roofed) with a single capstone. No mortar was used in their

Clochán or 'beehive hut'

construction. No-one knows for sure what their purpose was, or even who built them: perhaps they were pre-Christian shepherds or settlers, or pagan or medieval pilgrims visiting Mount Brandon. There are many fine examples dotted around Mount Eagle.

Oratories

These were small chapels, built as rectangular versions of clocháns. Like them, oratories were mortarless, relying on the stonemason's skill to select and shape the dry stones. Oratory construction was much more demanding, because the long curved side wall was prone to collapse. However, there is a perfect specimen at Gallarus, between Ballyferriter and Murreagh, only a few kilometres from the Way. Possibly the finest early Christian church in Ireland, it was built from local gritstone. Despite some 13 centuries of buffeting by Atlantic weather, it is still as waterproof as when it was built.

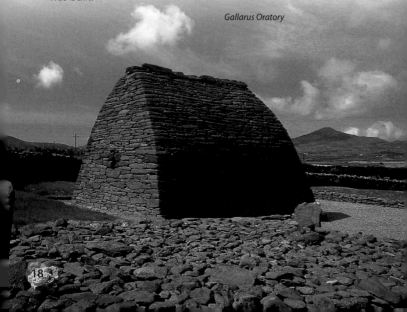

Gallarus Oratory

2·2 History and culture

Ireland's long history is marked by key events, including Viking raids, the Anglo-Norman settlement, forfeiture of lands to the English, suppression of Catholicism, the mid-19th century famine and emigration to the New World, the struggle for independence and the rise of the modern Irish state. All of these impinged, to a greater or lesser extent, on the Dingle peninsula. This section focuses on two features that are of particular relevance to walkers: the Gaeltacht and the pilgrimage tradition.

The Gaeltacht

Through all this, the Irish language at first flourished, later was almost silenced, then more recently was revived, celebrated and protected by legislation. Today the western Dingle peninsula, together with some other parts of western Ireland (notably Donegal and Mayo), is part of the stronghold known as the Gaeltacht – the areas where Irish is spoken and Irish culture is honoured. Its boundary is marked as a broad yellow north-south line just east of Lispole on Discovery sheet 70: west of that line OSi is not allowed to show placenames in English. Irish, a Celtic language, is officially the country's primary language, and is taught in all schools.

In Irish, the Dingle peninsula is called *Chorca Dhuibhne* (and the Dingle Way *Slí Chorca Dhuibhne*), perpetuating the name used in early Christian time by people who knew Duibhne as as a mythical goddess. (For help with pronunciation of this and other names, see inside our back cover.)

Some schools are Irish-medium and attract special funding and prestige. Government grants help Gaelic-speakers' businesses. Concerts of traditional music are regularly held in pubs and elsewhere. Radio and TV broadcasts are made in Irish, and Dingle's variant of Irish is regarded as particularly attractive and melodious. However, tourism is very important, and English is spoken to visitors.

Brendan Voyage memorial, Brandon Creek

Naomhógs (traditional leather boats) are still made at Scraggane

Saint Brendan (AD 484-577), the patron saint of mariners, travellers and whales, is one of Ireland's best-known saints and a strong presence on the Dingle peninsula. Born near Tralee, he was ordained in AD 512 and spent much of the rest of his extraordinarily long life travelling and working as a missionary around Ireland, in western Scotland, and most likely in Wales and western Europe. He built a monastic cell close to Brandon Mountain and established small chapels at Gallarus and Kilmalchedor (north-west of Dingle).

Brendan the Voyager (his secular title) is best known for his famous sea voyages in search of the 'Promised Land of the Saints' (also called 'the Isles of the Blessed'). Along with about 17 monks, he set sail from Brandon Creek in a traditional boat made of leather stretched on a wooden frame. In Ireland this is called a curragh, but in Dingle it is known as a *naomhóg* (pronounced 'nay-vogue'). According to tradition, Brendan reached the Americas by the 'stepping stone' route, via Scotland's Outer Hebrides, the Faroe Islands, Iceland and then Newfoundland – and back. A written account of his epic journey, Navigatio Sancti Brendani Abbatis first appeared sometime between the 8th and 11th centuries; it was translated into several languages and circulated widely in Europe. Brendan later established a monastery at Clonfert in south Galway, and was buried there.

In 1976, adventurer Tim Severin and his companions set out from Brandon Creek to test whether in Brendan's time it would have been possible to sail across the Atlantic in a leather boat. Their purpose-built naomhóg was 36 feet long and 8 feet abeam. Like Brendan's original boat, it was built of oxhide tanned in a traditional oak bark mixture, smeared with wool grease and flax, on a timber frame. His book *The Brendan Voyage* is an enthralling account of his journeys, spread over two seasons: see page 70. The memorial to this voyage shown on page 19 is a bronze sculpture depicting a much smaller boat. Next to it, the stone-carved inscription can be translated freely as *'Relax and don't panic'*.

2·3 Geology and scenery

Eons ago, in the area which is now south-west Ireland, volcanic activity thrust the sea bed above the water and left behind deposits of volcanic ash. These now constitute the oldest rocks on the Dingle peninsula, visible in the cliffs at Ballydavid Head on the north-west coast. About 400 million years ago sediments were laid down in the south-west and what we now call old red sandstone was formed. Sea levels

Rugged sandstone scenery on the descent from Brandon Mountain

and temperatures then rose and shellfish proliferated in the warm sea. When the sea eventually retreated, the shellfish skeletons turned into limestone which settled as a layer on top of the sandstone.

Next came a mountain building era, 340-280 million years ago. The sandstones and limestones were squashed, bent and pushed up, then eroded by wind and water, and the limestone all but disappeared. High parallel sandstone ridges took shape, one of which was the Dingle peninsula, aligned pretty well east-west, as is its peak-studded spine. Baurtregaum (851 m) is the highest summit in the Slieve Mish ridge in the east; Mount Eagle (516 m) guards the spine's westernmost end. The Brandon range, terminating in the dramatic cliffs of Brandon Head and topped by the highest peak, Brandon Mountain (952 m), is a northward extension, from near the town of Dingle.

The approach to Dunquin harbour

Typical coastal cliffs near Clogher

The land-forms we walk among today are largely the product of a series of Ice Ages, interspersed with warmer times, which occurred from about 200 million years ago to just 20,000 years ago. Glaciers gouged out and deepened valleys and chiselled them into U-shaped profiles. They also created corries – small bowl-shaped valleys at their heads: there are fine examples south-east of Brandon Mountain. They smoothed and sculpted the higher ground to produce rounded, rolling hills. The domed grassed-over hummocks you see in wide valleys are moraine heaps – the stones, silt and gravel left behind as the glaciers retreated. As the last Ice Age faded away, the land now lying beneath Dingle and Tralee Bays was flooded and the present coastline emerged, as did the Blasket Islands and their neighbours out in the Atlantic to the south-west.

Much later, tombolos – long fingers of land, for example at Inch on the south coast and extending north from Castlegregory (the Maharees) – were formed. One-time islands became joined to the mainland by bars built up from sand blown towards the shore from the islands.

Looking along the spine of Great Blasket

2·4 Habitats and wildlife

The Dingle Way
passes through a
range of habitats,
described below:

• uplands • woodlands
• hedgerows and fields
• wetlands • coasts.

Birds and mammals are most active at the beginning and the
end of the day, so you're most likely to see them if you start very early
or wander in the evening. Midges also follow this pattern, so cover up and
apply a repellent between May and September. Take binoculars along if
possible.

Uplands

Three types of heather dominate the moors: bell heather, with deep purple
flowers, the pink-flowering ling, and cross-leaved heath, usually pale pink.
Stunted clumps of yellow-flowering gorse may be dotted about (especially
on Mount Eagle). Masses of bog cotton, with downy white flower heads,
flourish in watery places where you'll also find insect-eating butterworts
and sundews. Purple moor-grass is widespread, forming dense tussocks
on damp moorland; it turns brown in late autumn and comes to life again
during spring. Skylarks and meadow pipits soar high overhead filling the
air with their melodious songs, while the calls of black ravens and choughs
are more raucous. Look out for kestrels hovering overhead and the darker,
fast-flying peregrine falcons. On lower ground you may also see and hear
curlews, with their long curved bill and plaintive call.

Oystercatcher feeding on shellfish

Woodlands

Native woodlands are few; one of the most extensive is a fine stand of prickly, dark green-leaved holly and taller, grey-barked birch around the old settlement of Killelton near Camp village. Conifer plantations are confined mainly to sheltered ground west of Cloghane.

Hedgerows and fields

In spring and summer, hedgerows (marking ancient field boundaries and roadsides) display a wealth of wildflowers. Dense blackthorn (which flowers in March) and hawthorn (blossoming white in May/June) are most prominent, entwined with clematis and honeysuckle. They in turn shelter yellow primroses, pink and white wild dog rose, yellow-flowering cowslip, aromatic yarrow, foxgloves with pinkish-purple, tubular flowers and creeping thistle. Vivid scarlet and purple fuchsia has spread vigorously since being introduced from New Zealand in the 19th century. You may be lucky enough to spot black medick, similar to clover and the source of Ireland's famous emblem, the shamrock; it has yellow flowers that turn into black pods in late summer.

Several small birds make their homes in hedgerows. Look out for the tiny, energetic russet-brown wren, robins with their red chests, blackbirds and song thrushes. Distinctive and noisy black and white magpies with their long black tails are easily spotted in fields and gardens.

Wildflowers flourish in hedgerows, including primroses (top)

Wren

Wetlands

The sheltered, shallow salt waters of Dingle's bays and harbours are havens for a host of birds: noisy black-backed oystercatchers, ringed plovers, with their curious stop-start motion, and redshanks trailing their red legs behind them in flight.

Yellow flag iris is widespread

Several species prefer freshwater habitats. Mallards are the most common of ducks, the drakes distinguished by their glossy dark green heads. Grey herons stand stock still for long periods in sheltered reaches. Mute swans (distinguished from whooper and bewick swans by their orange bill) glide about. Flocks of black-headed brent geese winter here, arriving in August. Yellow flag iris is prolific around pond margins, and purple loose-strife with long, dark pink flowers is common on marshy ground.

Coasts

Look out for common and grey seals, and the occasional dolphin. Out to sea, yellow-headed gannets plunge arrow-like into the waves to fish. Black cormorants are distinguished from shags by a white face-patch, and both stand on rocks with wings outspread to dry. Identify fulmars by their stiff-winged flight close to cliffs, where black-caped guillemots breed in dense colonies. Grey-backed herring gulls and the larger great black-backed gulls are common, not only on the coast but almost wherever they can scavenge food.

Redshank

Young grey seal in coastal surf

Flowering thrift (sea pink) clings to the cliff tops. Marram grass binds sand dunes, and in grasslands used for grazing (machair), wild flowers are amazingly plentiful. Early purple orchids, yellow-flowering bird's foot trefoil and thick mats of scented wild thyme bring splashes of colour in early summer.

Thrift flourishes on the cliffs near Clogher Head

2·5 The Blasket Islands

View north-west towards Brandon Mountain from Great Blasket

The Blaskets lie on the westernmost edge of Europe. They were inhabited for many centuries, probably since the Iron Age. Great Blasket, by far the largest of the six, had a population of some 160 people during World War I, but this soon dwindled and the island was finally abandoned in 1953.

Although geologically continuous with Dunmore Head, the archipelago for thousands of years has been separated from the mainland by Blasket Sound – a narrow but treacherous strip of water. This created the extreme isolation of these islands, making them a time capsule.

Even in the 20th century, island life had a distinctive, medieval flavour: arranged marriages, no machinery or electricity, and a cashless, co-operative economy. The abandoned village and outlying buildings add a fascinating human dimension to a walk that is already rich in mountain views, seascapes and wildlife. If you are lucky enough to enjoy a fine day on Great Blasket, it could be the highlight of your visit to Dingle. If the ferry cannot land, be sure to visit the Great Blasket Centre: see page 49.

Ruined house in the upper village

A day walk on Great Blasket (An Blascaod Mór)

Arriving at Great Blasket by ferry, via tender

Of all the islands, Great Blasket is the least inaccessible: see panel. Be prepared for wet and windy conditions: the boat crossing can be rough, and the island offers no trees, bushes or natural shelter. Take food and drink and make a day of it. On a clear day, the views are glorious, and the modest climb to the Cró (292 m) is rewarded by a unique panorama. In poor weather, the abandoned village is still of great interest, and its ruins offer some shelter. Of the few restored buildings, one may still house a café.

The walk itself resembles the Dingle Way in miniature: a leaf on a stem. From the harbour, you walk south-west along the spine of the island. The round trip to reach 'the Cró', (Croaghmore) is 7 km (4 miles) or about 2½ hours.

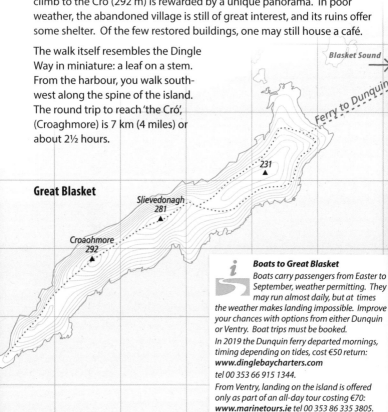

Blasket Sound →

Ferry to Dunquin

231 ▲

Great Blasket

Slievedonagh
281 ▲

Croaohmore
292 ▲

Boats to Great Blasket

Boats carry passengers from Easter to September, weather permitting. They may run almost daily, but at times the weather makes landing impossible. Improve your chances with options from either Dunquin or Ventry. Boat trips must be booked.

In 2019 the Dunquin ferry departed mornings, timing depending on tides, cost €50 return: **www.dinglebaycharters.com** tel 00 353 66 915 1344.

From Ventry, landing on the island is offered only as part of an all-day tour costing €70: **www.marinetours.ie** tel 00 353 86 335 3805.

You could continue a further 2 km to the island's south-western tip, but don't take chances with your return boat trip: if you miss it, you could be stranded for days or weeks. Allow time also to explore the village and perhaps also for a trip to the beach (White strand/Trá bán).

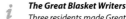

Start by climbing steeply through the village and at the top, turn right (westerly) along a grassy road. After 250 m, the road swings sharply left. To visit White Strand, where seals bask on the sand and play offshore, turn right instead down a path. After 1 km of path, you reach Sorrowful Cliff. In the 1830s, the wives of fishermen watched from here as the boats below were smashed in a sudden storm that killed 14 men.

Soon afterwards, you reach the junction with your return route: islanders ironically called this the 'traffic lights'. Bear right along the road, which starts to climb steeply and peters out. The remains of Doon Fort are a short detour to the right.

Continue to climb south-westerly to reach Slievedonagh (281 m). It commands fine views north to Inishtooskert, north-west to Mount Brandon and the Three Sisters, west to Mount Eagle and Dunmore Head, south to the Iveragh peninsula and south-west to the outlying smaller Blaskets. Descend the path south-westerly, then ascend the Cró, en route passing small clocháns, with ventilation holes for drying turf. The panorama from the Cró is even more impressive.

Depending on the weather and time available, either continue south-west to explore the island's south-westerly tip, or turn back to retrace your steps as far as the 'traffic lights'. Instead of going straight ahead, bear right to complete your circuit and follow the road back towards the village.

Picnic at the Cró, summit of Great Blasket

Distance 18·4 km 11·4 miles
Terrain roadside and canalside paths, minor road, moorland path – often rocky, occasionally boggy, with a boreen to finish
Grade steepish climb from Blennerville to moorland path, undulating path, then a steady descent to Camp (total ascent 200 m)
Food and drink Tralee (wide choice), Blennerville and Camp
Side trip Blennerville Windmill Visitor Centre
Summary easy walking from Tralee to beyond Blennerville, then a long, scenic traverse of the lower slopes of the Slieve Mish, with superb views across Tralee and west towards Brandon

km 0				18·4
3·0		7·7		7·7
Tralee	1·9 Blennerville	4·8	Derryquay River	4·8 Camp

Although Tralee was established by the Normans in 1216, it was razed during disturbances in the late 16th century and then by Cromwell's forces. It developed into a thriving commercial town in the 18th and 19th centuries and is now the capital (population 24,000) of county Kerry. It has held the Rose of Tralee festival annually in August since 1959.

The Thomas Ashe Memorial Hall (*Halla Tómas Ágas*) honours Ireland's first hunger striker, who died in 1917 during the struggle for Irish independence. This also houses the Kerry County Museum, open from Tuesday to Saturday year-round and daily from June to August: admission cost €5 in 2019: *www.kerrymuseum.ie*. It also houses Tralee's Tourist Information Centre, which is open 9.00 to 17.00 daily except Sundays.

- The Way starts on the western side of the Ashe Memorial Hall (see plan), where a Dingle Way signboard for the Way stands close to the fence. Go through a nearby gate and follow the path westward to the far side of the Green.

- Exit through a gate and turn left into Prince's Street; cross over, turning left (south). The road soon becomes Prince's Quay. Walk south to a roundabout, turn right, and continue beside the N86.

- Turn first right up Basin View, then left along the canalside path, which leads south-west for 1·6 km. Turn left at a road and cross bridges over the canal and River Lee.

Ashe Memorial Hall, Tralee

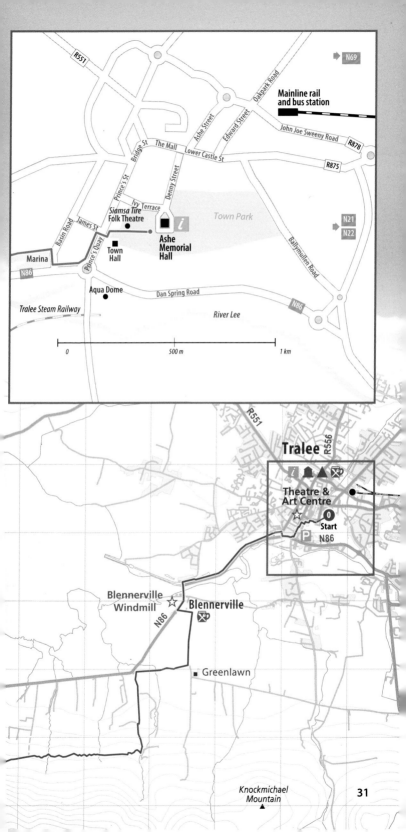

Tralee

Mainline rail and bus station

Siamsa Tíre Folk Theatre
Town Hall
Ashe Memorial Hall
Aqua Dome
Marina
Town Park
River Lee
Tralee Steam Railway
Dan Spring Road
Ivy Terrace
Denny Street
Prince's St
Bridge St
The Mall
Lower Castle St
Ashe Street
Edward Street
Oakpark Road
John Joe Sweeny Road
James St
Basin Road
Prince's Quay

R551
N69
R878
R875
N21
N22
N86

0   500 m   1 km

Theatre & Art Centre
Start
N86
Blennerville Windmill
Blennerville
Greenlawn
Knockmichael Mountain
R551
R556

31

River Lee and Tralee Ship Canal at Blennerville

- Windmill Lane is on your right: visit this historic windmill if time allows: see page 33. Afterwards continue south on the N86, and 230 m after Windmill Lane turn left to follow a minor road east (signposted Dingle Way).

- After 210 m turn right (south) to reach another junction after 800 m. Turn right again for a further 800 m to a junction where the Way turns left. Continue uphill for 1·3 km to a sharp bend where the road crosses a stream (km 6).

- Leave the road and go through a gate on the right to follow a path – there ar stepping stones over the boggy ground. Soon you come to the noticeboard for the Tonavane Walk, south of the Way.

- Cross three small streams, then climb gradually for nearly 2 km to cross the Curraheen River by a narrow bridge. (Shortly before, a signpost points north the main road, 1·5 km away.) The Way undulates for another 2·4 km to the bridge over the Derryquay River, tumbling through narrow clefts.

- Beyond the bridge, the Way rises slightly, then turns sharp left, climbing for a while, with views opening up westward. The path descends slightly to cross small stream. Cross two stiles, then the bridge over the Derrymore River.

- Bear left uphill through a gate to a stretch of railway sleepers and stepping stones. After a slight rise (where a 2-km path leads to the main road) the Wa continues rockily, overlooking Derrymore Strand. Go down and up again to stile and a bend in the minor road at Killelton.

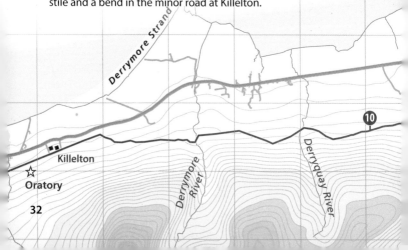

- Continue straight on past some houses. At a right bend, go through a small gate to a grassy path (the old Tralee-Dingle road), passing the ruins of several stone cottages. About 200 m from a stile, a stone path leads left to the carefully preserved remains of Killelton church.

- Back on the track, lined with holly and birch, you soon cross the first of three stiles, and then a tumbling stream. Over the next 700 m, negotiate another four stiles to reach a tarmac road.

i

Blennerville Windmill and Visitor Centre

This is the largest working windmill in Ireland (or Britain). If the wind is suitable, you may be lucky enough to see its tan sails driving the machinery. Built by the local landlord around 1800, it worked for a while, then lay derelict for over a century.

Its restoration in the 1980s was an ambitious community enterprise. The exhibition explains not only windmill construction, but also the role of Blennerville as the port of Tralee, and point of departure of the mid-19th century emigrant ships. You can also explore the five floors of the windmill itself. Open daily April to October 10.00-17.30, tel 353 66 712 1064: admission €7: www.blennerville-windmill.ie.

Blennerville Windmill ☆ **Blennerville** ⊠

N86

■ Greenlawn

Knockmichael Mountain ▲

- Follow the road for 30 m to a fork; the road to the right leads down to the N86 and Lower Camp, with pubs whose names (Junction Bar and Railway Tavern) recall the former railway: see page 69. To keep to the Way, bear left along the track, which soon traverses a crest.

- Descend and cross a minor road, and keep on downhill; to the right is the route of the former Tralee to Dingle railway.

- Cross the road; a sign warns walkers to detour via Camp village if the Finglas River is in spate – an extra 2 km. Normally, you drop down to the river and hop across large stepping stones, with a rope handrail for comfort.

Stepping stones across Finglas River

- A grassy track leads up to an intersection where Dingle Way signposts point in three directions (km 18·5). Turn right to reach Upper Camp after 1 km.

3·2 Camp → Annascaul
An Com → Abhainn an Scáil

Distance 15·7 km 9·8 miles

Terrain old, disused road across moorland and through small conifer plantation; short road walk, then boreens and minor roads through farmland; 3 km road walk to Annascaul village

Grade steepish climb from Finglas River valley to the col (235 m); undulating ascent from Inch to Maum; finally downhill to Annascaul (total ascent 270 m)

Food and drink Camp, Inch Strand and Annascaul

Summary across a low pass to the Dingle peninsula's south side, with superb views of Inch Strand, Castlemaine Harbour and the Iveragh peninsula mountains, to the lovely village of Annascaul

```
18·4                        7·2                    5·5      34·1
○──────────●────────────────────────────●──────────────────○
Camp  3·0  Knockbrack  4·5        Inch   3·4        Annascaul
      1·9                                5·5
```

- From Upper Camp on the N86, go 1 km south on the road between the Catholic church and Ashe's pub to return to the three-way junction at km 18·5.

- Bear right to climb fairly steeply for over 2 km to the col (235 m/770 ft above sea level).

- Just beyond the col, bear left at the Knockbrack junction, and descend the upper Emlagh River valley, with the western outliers of the Slieve Mish Mountains to your left.   Notice signs of peat being cut for fuel, with low cuttings carved into the moorland and banks of stacked peats left to dry.

- About 5 km beyond the pass, the road goes through a small conifer plantation, then descends to a Y-junction where you bear left. Bear in mind that vehicles also use this road.

- Cross the Emlagh River by a bridge, and within 300 m at a junction cross the road and continue uphill on a gravel track.

Inch Strand

- Beyond two modern houses go through a gate and, ascending slightly, follow a rough boreen, then descend, passing through a gate. The views of the long sweep of Inch Strand are superb.

- Soon, join a rough narrow rocky path, which may be boggy, and climb a stile. A path leads for about 60 m to join a vehicle track which continues westerly.

- After about 150 m, a minor road bears off to the left. Take this if you wish to descend all the way to Inch Strand (with a shop, café, and toilets, and a pub nearby).

Annascaul River

N86

N86

Annascaul

R561

▲ Doorah

▲ Knocknanacree

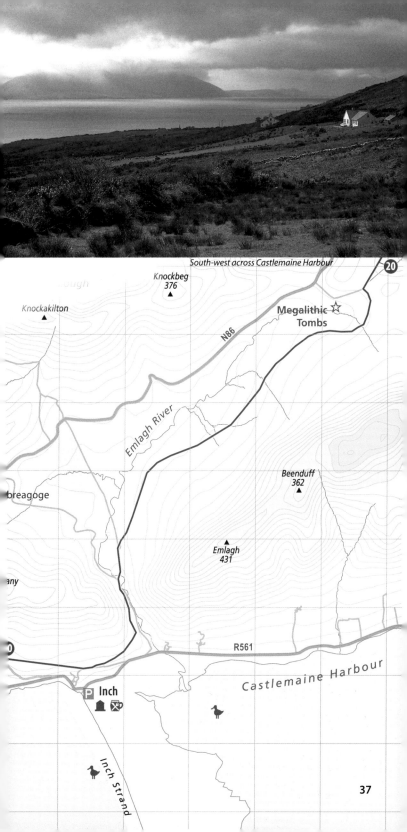

Knockbeg
376

Knockakilton

Megalithic Tombs ☆

N86

Emlagh River

Beenduff
362

breagoge

Emlagh
431

any

R561

Castlemaine Harbour

P **Inch**

Inch Strand

Across Dingle Bay to the Iveragh peninsula

- After Inch, the Way continues west on a rising track before descending to a tarmac road. Follow the road for 200 m, then continue along a boreen, gradually climbing.

- About 300 m further on, cross a stile and go through a gate. The track swings north-west to cross two roads; narrowing to a boreen, it leads unswervingly up to a junction where you bear left.

- The road swings right and descends directly to the village of Annascaul; there's a large standing stone in a field on the right.

- The South Pole Inn is well worth a visit for its Tom Crean legacy: see panel. Nearby is a bronze statue of Crean holding two of his beloved sled pups, erected in 2003.

> *i* **Tom Crean** (1877-1938) was born in Gurtacurrane, 3 km from Annascaul. He distinguished himself in Sir Robert Scott's two Antarctic expeditions (1901-04,1912) and was a heroic member of Ernest Shackleton's expedition in 1914-1916. An Antarctic mountain and glacier are named after him. He was a modest man, reluctant to speak of his explorations. He settled at Annascaul after serving in World War 1, and opened the South Pole Inn in 1927.
>
> The pub had mixed fortunes after 1948 and was closed for many years, but in the 1990s it was refurbished. It displays memorabilia of Crean's visits to Antarctica. Today, it serves meals and sells souvenirs: tel 353 66 915 7388. For Smith's biography of Crean, see page 70.

The South Pole Inn, Annascaul

3·3 Annascaul → Dingle

Abhainn an Scáil → Daingean Uí Chúis

36 40 41

Distance	22·5 km 14·0 miles
Terrain	undulating minor roads through farmland to Lispole; farm boreens and field paths across hillsides; vehicle track and roads to Dingle
Grade	steady climbs from Annascaul, northwards from Minard Castle, and from Lispole to the Connor Pass road (total ascent 340 m)
Food and drink	Annascaul, Lispole (garage) and Dingle (wide choice)
Summary	quiet country roads lead to a picturesque cove and Minard Castle ruin; more scenic quiet roads inland to Lispole then north towards the mountains and excellent wide vistas; final descent to beckoning Dingle in its sheltered harbour

```
34·1     5·5              5·5                  7·5                    4·0    56·6
 ○────────●────────────────●──────────────────────────────────────●────────○
Annascaul  3·4 Minard Castle 3·4 Lispole        4·7        Garfinny River 2·5 Dingle
```

- From the Annascaul River bridge, follow the main road south-west, away from the village. After 250 m, turn left (towards Inch and Killarney). After a further 450 m, turn right off the main road, up a minor road which you follow for over 4 km to the coast.

- The road climbs the shoulder of Doorah to a height of 110 m. It then descends to reach a small sandy cove fringed by smooth shingle. It is overlooked by the gaunt remains of Minard Castle, a tower house built in the 16th century but partly destroyed by Cromwell's forces in 1650. It's best viewed from the beach: entry to the fenced grounds is prohibited.

- At the western end of the cove, fork left, then almost immediately right. (A signposted path leads a short way from here to Tobar Eoin Baiste – St John the Baptist's well – a puddle surrounded by a low wall, backed by a small stone carved with a cross).

- Farm tracks and then a minor road take you north-west and uphill, past junctions on the left and right and across a dip.

- The Way starts to climb again, and turns left along a hedged lane above a house. Continue to a T-junction, turn right and climb steeply.

Minard Castle

Lispole Church

- At an apparent fork, pass a white farmhouse on the right and the adjacent Aglish burial grounds. Go up to an intersection and turn right, then soon left at a T-junction (km 42·8).

- Descend and turn left to leave the road where it bends right. (If instead you stay on the road and take the first turn left, you may find a café.) The minor road loses height steadily, and there is an impressive viaduct in fields to the right, a relic of the former railway. Pass through the hamlet of Lispole (*Lios Póil*) on the busy N86; its garage may have snacks.

- Waymarking along the next 5 km towards the Garfinny River is sparse, so care is needed. Follow the N86 west for about 150 m, over the Owenalondrig River, and almost immediately go right. Continue directly north for nearly 1 km, soon gaining height. Fork left, and follow a minor road north-westwards for 1·4 km.
- Turn right where the half-hidden waymarker points to a stile, taking you into a field. Walk uphill beside the dyke to another stile and bear left. The superb view extends south-west to the Iveragh peninsula and, out to sea, to the spires of Skellig Michael. A boreen leads past a house with very noisy dogs (locked up) and a large farmhouse at Lisdargan.
- Turn right at a junction, and after about 50 m turn left along a farm track to a bridge and cross the stream. Walk across rough pasture to another stile. Continue parallel to the gorse-crested dyke. Go through a gap between two walls, now with the dyke on your right, then through another gap to a path, which leads to a vehicle track.
- Keep right of a stone building; beyond a fence turn right. Cross a stile on the left, traverse the field to another stile, then keep close to the dyke on the right.
- Bear slightly right to join a track between dykes for about 200 m to an obscure low stile. Cross it to continue along the track (which may be very muddy) and pass over a small stile by a gate.
- Pass a farmhouse and go diagonally left to follow a rough road around bends to a T-junction. Turn right and then left to follow a farm track, with a painted house above right.

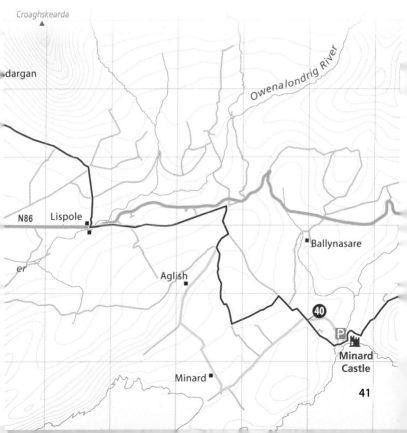

Dingle fishing port and harbour

- After another 50 m, go through a gateway and turn right uphill on a stony track. Bend left through a gate; cross the lower field edge to a stile and continue along the bottom of another field.

- Go through a gateway to a lane and follow it for a short distance to the next gate. The lane leads to a tarmac road, which you follow for about 200 m to a sharp left bend, then go right along a rough track.

- The track skirts the hillside and takes you over a solid bridge spanning the Garfinny River, to a tarmac road where you turn left.

- The road rises to cross the Connor Hill road, then descends towards Dingle. The track soon becomes a road, and after more than 1 km it reaches the edge of Dingle, where it becomes Spa Road.

- Take the roadside path into town, soon reaching Main Street, where you'll see Way signposts. Bear slightly left, then right, and walk down The Mall to a roundabout. Turn right along The Tracks, past fishing quays to Strand Street. Bear left for about 100 m to Dingle's Tourist Information Centre in Strand Street.

Dingle

The town area has been occupied since prehistoric times when the Celts built a fort here. Under the Anglo-Normans it developed as a walled town. Strong trading links were made with France (through Brest) and with Spain (La Coruña).

Statue of Fungie

In the late 16th century the English took control and excise officers were appointed to try to extract taxes from illegal wine importers.

Traditionally a fishing and market town, tourism is now Dingle's main source of income, enhanced by the shooting of the film '*Ryan's Daughter*' in the area in 1969: see page 48. Fungie, an agile and sociable dolphin, arrived in 1983, and boosted tourism further with boat trips that guaranteed sightings: see *www.dingledolphin.com*. Although some claim to recognise his dorsal fin, he is getting implausibly old for a dolphin and some people suspect that the original animal has a successor. Dingle has a wide range of shops, cafés, pubs and restaurants, with plenty of accommodation. Its population of 2000 is greatly swollen in season by tourism.

Dingle town shop fronts

43

3·4 Dingle → Dunquin
Daingean Uí Chúis → Dún Chaoin

Distance	22·4 km 13·9 miles
Terrain	undulating roads to Ventry, then beach walking; vehicle tracks and boreens across shoulder of Mount Eagle; main road past Slea Head and minor road into Dunquin
Grade	minor climb to reach Ventry, some stiff climbing around the shoulder of Mount Eagle, with gentler gradients thereafter (total ascent 370 m)
Food and drink	Dingle, Ventry, Dunquin (various)
Side trip	Mount Eagle, Great Blasket Centre (see page 49)
Summary	from tranquil Ventry, a fine beach walk leads up to a varied traverse of the shoulder of Mount Eagle, with magnificent views of the dramatic coastline

56·6   8·4   10·0   4·0   79·0

Dingle   5·2   **Ventry**   6·2   **Slea Head** 2·5 **Dunquin**

- Set out from Dingle's Tourist Information Centre along the roadside footpath and follow it past the marina to a roundabout.

- Turn left along the R559 road, cross the bridge and walk up the road, keeping straight on at the first junction (signed for Ventry/Ceann Trá). About 300 m further on, bear right at a fork and continue west along the minor road through undulating countryside.

- Three km after the fork the Way turns off to follow two sides of a triangle to reach Ventry. (If in a hurry, you could save 2·2 km by staying on the road instead to reach Ventry directly: skip to page 46.)

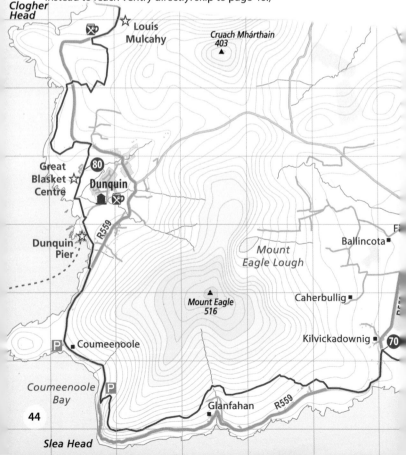

Across Ventry Harbour to Mount Eagle

- To stay on the Way, turn right at some houses (km 61·6), then left through a gate to follow a cattle-trod boreen – very muddy at first, albeit partly relieved by duckboards.

- As you gain height, look behind for views over Ventry Harbour. Emerge at the top through a gate, and turn sharp left to descend the minor road for 1·3 km. Turn right at the T-junction to rejoin the road you left.

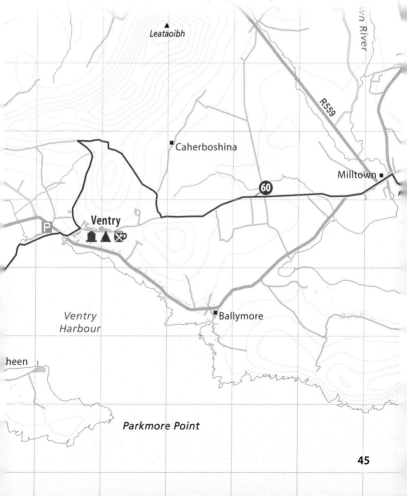

- Descend past the school for 200 m into Ventry. If you're planning to stay at Dunquin's hostel, stock up here: Dunquin has no shops.
- Cross the main road (R559) just beyond the Ventry Inn, and follow the waymarker pointing down a narrow path to the beach.
- Turn right to follow the Way along the beach for the next 2·5 km, its firm sand making excellent walking. (A car park information board covers local sea birds and habitats.) If the small stream is too deep to paddle across, use the bridge near the top of the beach.
- Cross the stream towards the southern end of the beach by way of two narrow bridges. At km 68, look for the waymarker pointing right up a sandy track leading inland from the beach.
- At a junction, turn left along a tarmac road for 140 m. Turn right, then right again, following the tarmac.
- At the end of the tarmac, bear left down a short boreen in front of a farmhouse. Soon, turn sharp left along a very muddy path between tall hedgerows, narrow and overgrown in places. This rises gently, widens out and swings right to become a farm track that rises to meet the R559 main road at km 70.
- ⚠ Turn left to walk alongside the road (with care, heavy traffic in season). After 1 km, turn right up a loose-surfaced road that climbs steeply at first, then swings left toward a house. Turn right up a boreen with this house to its left and a stream to its right.
- This climb is steep at first, soon reaching a stone wall with gate and metal stile. After the wall, the gradient eases and the route swings left to follow a very fine drystone wall. This hillside is exposed, and you'll see various techniques used to stabilise the stones.

Coumeenoole Bay from the Way: see page 48

Clochán beside the Way

Behind you are fine views over Ventry and Dingle harbours. As you continue westward, you start to see the most southerly outliers of the Blasket Islands, followed by Great Blasket itself.

After cresting another ridge, you enter a wide valley, with an extraordinarily dense concentration of archaeological remains – over 500 features, including many clocháns.

Cross the watercourse on stepping stones: poles will be useful if it is in spate. The path undulates between stone-walled fields. As you pass above two modern houses, look for an intact clochán nearby.

The substantial dyke on your left turns hard left; instead, continue on a clear path through low gorse. Further on, the path bends right around the rocky shoulder of Mount Eagle. This section is littered with clocháns in various stages of collapse.

- Another climb, steep at first, ends at a dyke with stile. To continue the Way, cross the stile; to detour up Mount Eagle instead, see panel.

- Once over the stile, the Way descends steeply, following yellow-topped poles, to meet the R559 at km 76, north of Slea Head. Turn right and walk about 150 m to the car park.

- Follow the road north and north-west, directly above Coumeenoole Bay, overlooked by the jagged cliffs of Dunmore Head, the most westerly point of mainland Ireland. In the picnic area, a stone commemorates the 1969 filming of 'Ryan's Daughter'.

> ### Mount Eagle (516 m/1690 ft)
> Instead of crossing the stile, turn right to follow the line of the dyke uphill (north-east). With the dyke at first on your left, climb steeply over grass, then rocky ground. Further up, the gradient eases, and where the dyke dips briefly, cross it through an obvious gap but keep following its line. It veers north-east and becomes discontinuous, but leads you steadily uphill, climbing steeply.
> You reach almost level ground, and after the dyke peters out, short painted poles mark the last few hundred metres of very gentle ascent to the summit (with survey cairn). From here, the panorama includes Dingle, the Iveragh peninsula, Blasket Islands, Brandon Mountain and the Slieve Mish Mountains. Retrace your steps to rejoin the Way. Allow 2 to 2½ hours for the walk; total ascent is 360 m.

- The road leads north, slightly uphill, for over 1 km: look for where the Way turns left to follow a short path that emerges on a minor road.

Great Blasket (left) and Dunmore Head from the Way

Clocháns are abundant near Slea Head

- Turn right to follow the road past a cemetery, then at the next junction bear left. Soon you pass the access to Dunquin pier.

- Bear left at a fork down a gravel road, past deserted stone cottages to the shingle shore. Cross the stream by the steel bridge.

- Go uphill, passing (or visiting) the Great Blasket Centre: see panel. You arrive in Dunquin at a road junction.

i

Great Blasket Centre *(Ionad an Bhlascaoid Mhóir), Dunquin*
This radical building uses exciting techniques to reveal the Blasket heritage . A long interior corridor leads to a superb view of the island itself. Imaginative displays include scale models, multilingual film and exhibits about the islanders' lifestyle, literature and diaspora. There is a bookshop, research room and restaurant. The next best thing to a visit to the island, it shows how untouched by the 20th century life on Blasket was.
*Open daily from Easter to end October 10.00-18.00. In 2019, adult admission cost €5. Tel 353 66 915 6444, **www.blasket.ie**.*

Dunquin pier from above

Distance	**23·1 km** 14·4 miles
Terrain	**minor roads and boreens lead to a coastal path, then minor roads to fine beaches, a cliff-top path and more minor roads**
Grade	**steady ascent from Dunquin, then gentle gradients (total ascent 100 m**
Food and drink	**Dunquin, Murreagh, Ballydavid, Feohanagh**
Side trip	**Dún an Óir**
Summary	**an outstandingly scenic day with superb cliff-top stretches punctuated by a long beach walk with a rugged coastline**

79·0 — 5·7 — 6·0 — 6·3 — 5·1 — 102·1
Dunquin 3·5 **Colgher** 3·7 **Dún an Óir** 3·9 **Murreagh** 3·2 **Feohanagh**

Looking past Clogher beach to the Three Sisters and Ballydavid He...

50

- Walk north uphill from the Dunquin crossroads. Just around a wide bend, bear left along a gravel road, and immediately bear right to follow a rough track northwards.

- The track climbs across moorland, then descends to the main road. Turn right at the R559, and after 200 m pass a seasonal café: *www.tigaine.com*.

- Soon after Tig Aine, you reach the Louis Mulcahy Pottery: see panel. About 150 m after the pottery, turn left off the main road down a narrow lane.

- At a right bend, continue ahead on a grassy path with a stream on your left. Further on, go through sand dunes to overlook Clogher's beach.

- From the beach, for a scenic 2·8-km detour follow waymarkers west to An Drom, then turn north-east along the coast for nearly 1 km. Return south-east by a small lane to the main road and turn left to resume the Way: skip to page 52 bullet 2.

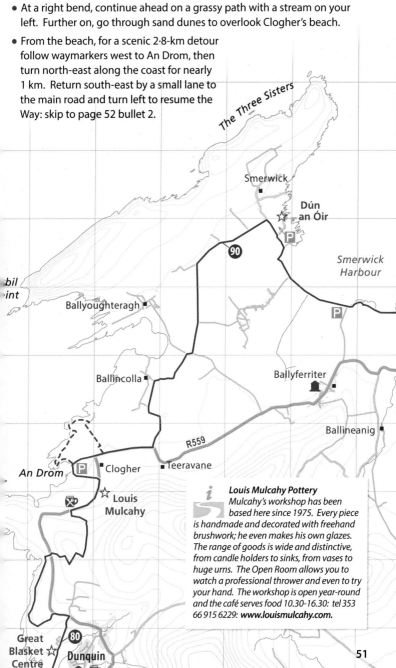

> ### *i* Louis Mulcahy Pottery
> *Mulcahy's workshop has been based here since 1975. Every piece is handmade and decorated with freehand brushwork; he even makes his own glazes. The range of goods is wide and distinctive, from candle holders to sinks, from vases to huge urns. The Open Room allows you to watch a professional thrower and even to try your hand. The workshop is open year-round and the café serves food 10.30-16.30: tel 353 66 915 6229: www.louismulcahy.com.*

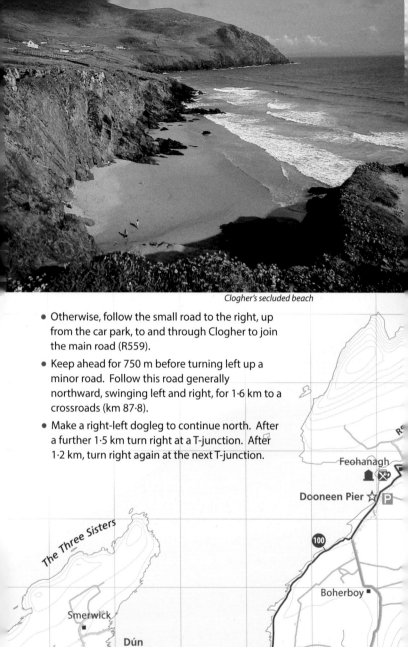

Clogher's secluded beach

- Otherwise, follow the small road to the right, up from the car park, to and through Clogher to join the main road (R559).

- Keep ahead for 750 m before turning left up a minor road. Follow this road generally northward, swinging left and right, for 1·6 km to a crossroads (km 87·8).

- Make a right-left dogleg to continue north. After a further 1·5 km turn right at a T-junction. After 1·2 km, turn right again at the next T-junction.

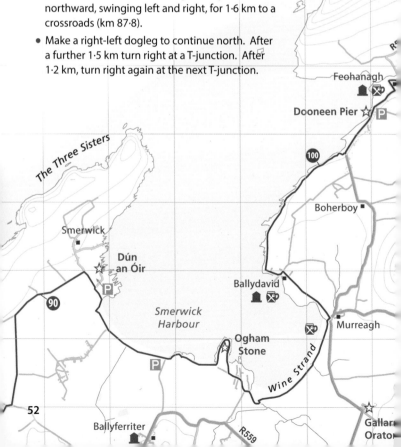

Feohanagh

Dooneen Pier ☆ P

100

The Three Sisters

Boherboy ■

Smerwick
■

Dún
an Óir
☆ P

Ballydavid ■

90

Smerwick
Harbour

Murreagh ■

Ogham
Stone ☆

Wine Strand

52

Ballyferriter

R559

Gallar
Orato

Dún an Óir promontory fort

Faha Ridge ▲

Ballinknockane ■

Ballycurrane ■

▲ Brandon Mountain 952

P

An Bóthar ■

■ Cuas

Kilquane ■

Feohanagh River

Ballinloghig ■

Rinn Chonaill ▲

An Scraig (676)

Beennal

Dún an Óir

This was originally an Iron Age promontory fort, reinforced in 1580 by a force of Italians and Spaniards who were assisting Irish rebels against English rule. About 600 soldiers were slaughtered after they surrendered to Lord Grey's English soldiers, although controversy has raged down the centuries as to whether Grey had promised to spare their lives or whether he intended the brutal measure to discourage future attempts at invasion via Ireland. A memorial was put up in 1980.

- Within 150 m, a sign invites you to turn left to visit Dún an Óir: see above. This short detour is worthwhile for its rich history, and wonderful views.

- After the fort, continue south-east towards Smerwick Harbour. The name is of Norse origin, from *smaor* (butter) and *vick* (harbour). Bear right along the beach, which gives easy walking on firm sand for 1·4 km.

- Just short of a small headland, leave the beach through a gap in the dunes and bear left along a cliff-top path. Follow the Way around the perimeter of the headland, on which stands a stone bearing the Ogham alphabet: see page 17.

Ogham stone on the headland

- After the headland, head south until you reach a tarmac road where you turn left. Follow it for 380 m through Wine Strand Holiday Homes, then turn left down a lane to reach the beach where you turn right.

- Cross the narrow girder bridge at the beginning, and soon after, cross a small stream. The next 2 km is on the firm sand of Wine Strand, its name recalling its history of smuggling. At its end, cross the broad stream on stepping stones and turn right along a gravel road towards the village of Murreagh.

- To reach Murreagh, bear right at a fork, then soon left. To stick to the Way, instead bear left and follow the minor coastal road for 1 km to the fishing port of Ballydavid.

Eroding coastline near the path

- Turn left to go through the village, which has pubs and also a spa offering local seaweed baths, en route for the sea shore, where you turn right.

- Shortly the tarmac gives way to a grassy path between a dyke and the cliff edge, for 2 km of coastal walking with magnificent views. In places the path comes very close to the brink, and care is needed.

- Soon after passing the second of two communications masts, you meet a road and bear left. After the viewpoint at Dooneen Pier, the road heads inland and through the tiny village of Feohanagh.

Crossing Smerwick Harbour towards Wine Strand

3·6 Feohanagh → Cloghane
An Fheothanach → An Clochán

Distance	25·7 km 16·0 miles
Terrain	minor roads; moorland and hillside paths, boggy in places; minor roads and finally a field path
Grade	flattish, then a steep climb to the col at 650 m, with a protracted descent, very steep at first; then a short climb, and a longer one towards Cloghane (total ascent 780 m excluding Brandon Mountain summit)
Food and drink	Feohanagh, Brandon and Cloghane
Side trips	Brandon Mountain (Cnoc Bréanainn)
Summary	the most dramatic and challenging day, crossing the shoulder of Brandon Mountain, descending to Brandon Bay, and finishing with easier going to the village of Cloghane

```
102·1                                                                          127·8
 O────────11·0────────●────────8·7────────●────────6·0────────○
Feohanagh  6·8   col (Brandon)  5·4       Brandon village 3·7  Cloghane
```

- The Way continues east through Feohanagh and after 200 m turns left before the school.

- After 300 m turn right up a green road which narrows to an overgrown boreen. Turn right along a track that swings downhill to the river. Walk upstream to the bridge, cross, and bear right up the road. Follow it to enter a field by a metal stile.

- The field section may be a bit boggy after wet weather and cattle traffic, though it is relieved by wooden planks. Finally you emerge on a muddy farm track and turn left at the R549 road. After 550 m, you pass An Bóthar, a splendid pub and B&B.

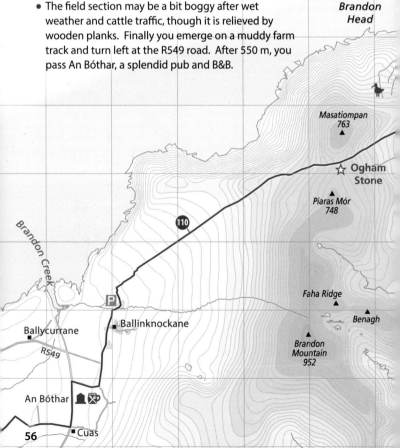

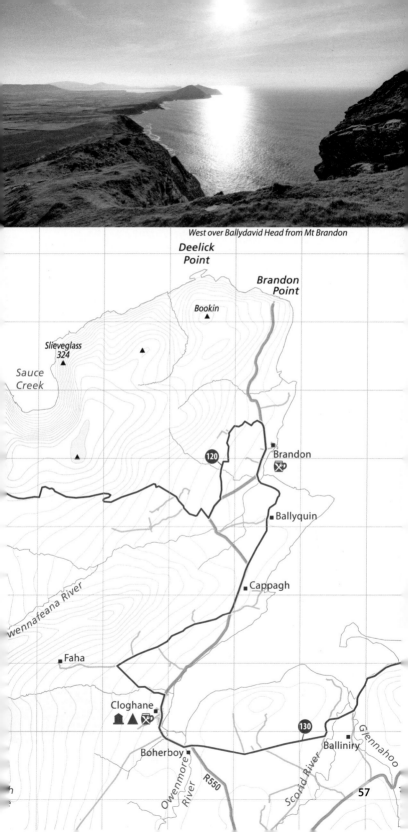

West over Ballydavid Head from Mt Brandon

Deelick
Point

Brandon
Point

Bookin ▲

Slieveglass
324
▲

▲

Sauce
Creek

▲

120

■ Brandon

■ Ballyquin

■ Cappagh

wennafeana River

■ Faha

Cloghane

130

■ Balliniry

Glennahoo

■ Boherboy

Owenmore
River

R550

Scord River

Masatiompan seen from the col

- About 150 m beyond An Bóthar, the Way turns right uphill. To detour first to Brandon Creek (*Cuas an Bhodaigh*) continue north on the road for a further 1 km. (See page 20 for the Brendan voyage.) Refer to the map to resume the Way afterwards, and skip the next bullet.

- After the Way turns right uphill, it passes another B&B on the left to reach a grassy triangle within 400 m. Turn left and after 400 m pass a minor road on the left.

- Continue to follow this road northward as it swings around farm buildings through various bends. It ends after a further 1·6 km, at a car park.

- Go through the gate on the car park's far side, and follow the vehicle track for only 110 m before turning right uphill. It's easy to overshoot this unmarked turn. Leave the track and follow the line of black waymarker posts heading north-eastward over open ground, uphill steeply at first.

- The gradient eases towards the middle of the ascent, where the track's origins – as an (unfinished) military road built by the English – are clearest. In poor weather you may be glad of the intermediate white marker posts.

- The final haul to the col (at 650 m/2135 ft) is particularly steep. You will see the pinnacle of Masatiompan (763 m) soaring above to your left, but the summit of Brandon is hidden, a few km away to your right.

- For directions to Brandon's summit, see below. Attempt it only in good visibility, and if carrying suitable equipment including a map and compass: see page 9.

Brandon Mountain

From the col, turn right uphill, keeping the fence on your left. Follow its line southwards as it climbs past first a small hump, then a larger one (Piaras Mór), on your right. Keep to the fence as it zig-zags up to a clearly defined ridge. As the ridge narrows, cross a stile and continue uphill, with the fence now on your right. Follow a clear path up a rocky stretch, then cross some level ground and a slight dip. Climb steeply, mostly on grass, then across some level ground with a stile over a fence. A final steady pull leads to the summit, with its wooden cross, monastic remains and cairn. The panorama takes in the Iveragh Peninsula to the south; Mount Eagle, Dunmore Head and the Blaskets to the south-west; Smerwick Harbour to the west; and Brandon and Tralee Bays to the east. (The white posts leading south-west mark the ascent route from An Baile Breac.) Retrace your steps northwards to the col. Allow 2½ to 3 hours from the col for the round trip (total ascent 300 m).

- At the col, use the stile to cross the fence, with a fine Ogham stone on its far side: see page 17.

- The rough path drops into the wide valley below, very steeply for the first 2 km. This section is treacherous: poles are strongly recommended, and during or after wet weather, take extreme care with the stream crossings and other obstacles.

- The gradient slackens after a while as the path descends a spur of Masatiompan, and drops steadily to meet a gravel road near a bridge. Go through a kissing-gate beside a locked gate.

Ogham stone at the col below Brandon Mountain

- Follow the gravel road for a further 4 km down into the valley of the Owennafeana River. After some shallow zigzags you finally reach tarmac. Follow the road as it bends sharp right to a junction where you turn left.

East over Brandon Bay from the cairn

- After 330 m, the Way turns left again (km 119·5). If instead you continue straight on, you will rejoin the Way near Brandon post office, saving 2 km of tarmac at the price of missing views of Brandon Bay.

- Meantime, the Way winds about above the village for about 1 km then turns right at a T-junction, and descends to the village from the north.

- Walk through Brandon village (*Cé Bhréanainn*), perhaps pausing at one of its pubs: Mullally's is on the main road, whereas Murphy's is on the pier. To resume the Way, just past the post office, turn sharp left along a lane for about 30 m, then go right along a raised, railed concrete path and bridge across the Owennafeana River.

- Negotiate a rocky bank and cross the rough grass to reach a road where you bear right. Go straight on at a junction to a crossroads: turn right. The road gains height steadily, through small conifer plantations.

- About 2 km from the crossroads, watch out for the left turn (km 126) down to Cloghane village, marked by a black post. Follow the path to a stile, then continue down on a clear path, crossing small bridges over channels. After about 300 m, cross the bridge over a stream fringed with holly and willow.

- Descend steeply to another bridge. The path swings right to a small gate, beyond which you bear left along a boreen. Walk past old Cloghane burial ground and the remains of a 13th century church, into Cloghane.

3·7 Cloghane → Castlegregory
An Clochán → Caisleán Ghriaire

Distance	26·4 km 16·4 miles
Terrain	quiet country roads, extended beach walking along shores of Brandon and Tralee Bays, quiet roads into Castlegregory
Grade	one minor climb out of Cloghane, otherwise flat
Food and drink	Cloghane, Fahamore and Castlegregory
Side trip	Dún an Óir
Summary	a long but not arduous day, dominated by Ireland's longest beach, with fine seascapes including the offshore Magharees

```
127·8   5·0            10·6              10·8        154·2
Cloghane  3·1 Fermoyle   6·6      Fahamore   6·7  Castlegregory
```

- Walk south through Cloghane and out into the countryside, soon crossing the Owenmore River on a quiet road which rises slightly to cross a broad peninsula.

- After about 3 km, you cross Scorid and Glennahoo Rivers, skirt the shore and turn left at a T-junction towards Fermoyle Strand. Go over a humpback bridge to a car park at the end of the tarmac. A few steps beyond, you reach a vast expanse of sand and sea.

- You are about to follow Ireland's longest beach all the way to Fahamore, some 11 km (6·8 miles). The beach should be safe to walk at all but the highest of spring tides, with the possible exception of an elongated shingle bank after about 4·5 km: if need be, take to the dunes or wait for a safe passage. Normally, you need to paddle across only a few small streams along the way.

- The beach is full of interest, with seaweed, shells, pebble drifts, crab skeletons, flotsam, birds (notably oystercatchers) and perhaps horses. It's fringed by scattered sand dunes, covered in wiry marram grass, with a backdrop of superb mountain views. Enjoy the extraordinary shape of the tombolo: see page 66. To its north are the Magharee Islands (Seven Hogs).

North-west across Brandon Bay

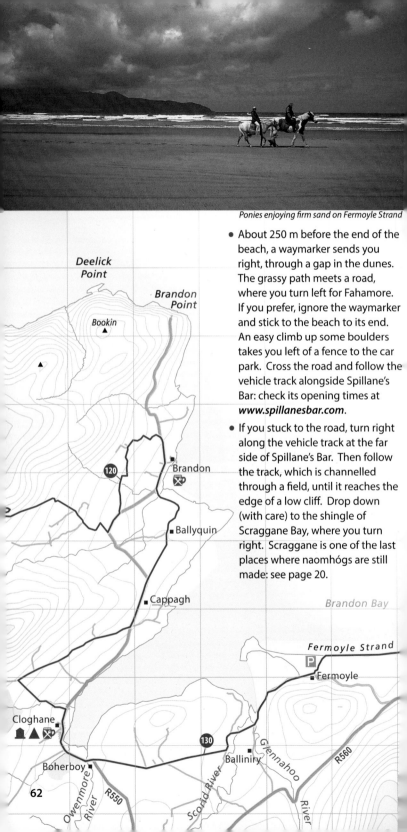

Ponies enjoying firm sand on Fermoyle Strand

- About 250 m before the end of the beach, a waymarker sends you right, through a gap in the dunes. The grassy path meets a road, where you turn left for Fahamore. If you prefer, ignore the waymarker and stick to the beach to its end. An easy climb up some boulders takes you left of a fence to the car park. Cross the road and follow the vehicle track alongside Spillane's Bar: check its opening times at *www.spillanesbar.com*.

- If you stuck to the road, turn right along the vehicle track at the far side of Spillane's Bar. Then follow the track, which is channelled through a field, until it reaches the edge of a low cliff. Drop down (with care) to the shingle of Scraggane Bay, where you turn right. Scraggane is one of the last places where naomhógs are still made: see page 20.

Deelick Point

Brandon Point

Bookin ▲

▲

120

Brandon

Ballyquin

Cappagh

Brandon Bay

Fermoyle Strand

P

Fermoyle

Cloghane

130

Balliniry

Glennahoo

R560

Boherboy

Owenmore River

R550

Scord River

River

- Continue along the field edges, past a shed and a white house. If the tide is in, follow the road parallel to the shore, otherwise take to the sand for about 1 km.

- Leave the beach at Kilshannig via a shingle ramp at the end of a low wall of boulders. (A short diversion left takes you to the ruined church at Kilshannig, which has a seventh century cross slab in its graveyard, carved with the Greek letters chi-rho which symbolise Christ.)

- Turn right for 25 m, then bear left along a track opposite a small white cottage. (This cottage is your landmark for a right turn if you've had to walk along the road.) Go straight ahead (south-east) to the next beach.

- Turn right along the sand, or walk along the fringing machair for a few hundred metres, to bypass a flat rocky outcrop. Follow the beach which now stretches southward for 2 km.

- Cross to a broad area of machair, returning briefly to the beach afterwards. Leave the beach by walking up a ramp just before its end.

- Continue south across the grass, along a path beside the road, then over more grass to a bridge across the Trench. Here, turn left as signed to return to the beach for 1·2 km. Turn right along the road for 600 m to reach Castlegregory, at a crossroads with Fitzgerald's shop on the corner.

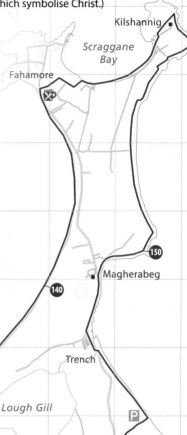

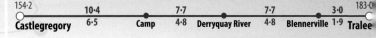
Distance **28·8 km 17·9 miles**

Terrain **quiet roads, beach walking, boreens, rough moorland track, finishing with canalside and roadside paths into Tralee**

Grade **steep climb from the beach through Camp village, another climb from Finglas River, then undulating moorland (total ascent 300 m)**

Food and drink **Castlegregory, Aughacasla, Lower and Upper Camp, Blennerville, Tralee**

Summary **after a final beach walk, the Way wends inland via Camp to cross the lower slopes of the Slieve Mish, down to Blennerville and back to Tralee**

154·2	10·4		7·7		7·7		3·0	183·0
○	6·5		4·8		4·8		1·9	○
Castlegregory		**Camp**		**Derryquay River**		**Blennerville**		**Tralee**

- The Way goes ahead and slightly left through Post Office Square to another crossroads, where Dingle Way signposts send you left along a minor road leading south-east.

- The tarmac ends after 2 km, giving way to gravel and sand. Cross the Owencashla River, and after 250 m follow the road as it bends right, now on tarmac again. After 450 m, pass the Anchor caravan park.

- Just afterwards, look out for the enigmatic Aughacasla stone standing in a field on the left. The stone itself is original, and it stands about 4 m tall, leaning and tapering. It has been raised onto steps and has had a cement effigy resembling a face added on top: see page 65.

- Keep straight on for a further 1 km to reach the R560 at the hamlet of Aughacasla.
- Turn left along the main road for 200 m, then turn left past a caravan and camping park to the beach, soon crossing a small stream.
- If the tide is in, you may have to leave the beach via a ramp, so as to bypass rocks further on. Walk around the field edges, keeping the fence on your left.
- After about 250 m this route starts to push you away from the beach: look for a rough gap in the brambles on the left, then negotiate a small stream and a channel and cross the field to regain the beach.
- Continue along the beach: you may have to wade the Meena-scarty River where it runs parallel to the shore, but the walking is wonderful.

The Aughacasla standing stone

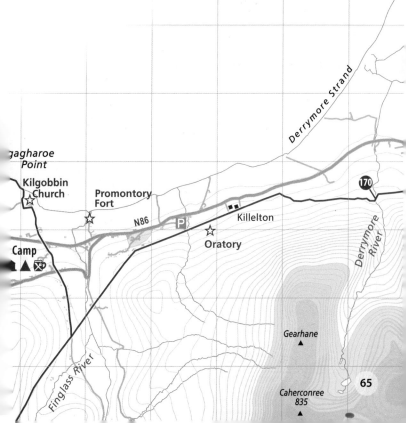

- Continue eastward, around the broad headland of Carrigagharoe Point. Just beyond it, turn right up a waymarked path through a gap in the low cliff looking for the church.

- Pass Kilgobbin Church, which dates from 1824, then follow the road as it bends left then right.

- Reach and cross the R560 at Lower Camp. Continue 500 m to the N86 main road, where you could catch a bus direct to Tralee.

- To complete the Way, continue for 1 km straight up the minor road, over the next crossroads at Upper Camp to reach the crossroads with Dingle Way signposts – the junction with your outward route: see page 34.

- Turn left and go down to cross the Finglas River by the stepping stones. Cross a tarmac road and follow a

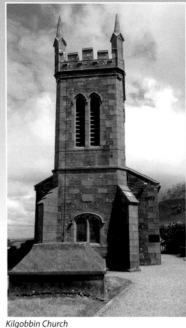

Kilgobbin Church

gravel road, and then pursue a boreen uphill. After you start to descend, with a white house in view, turn left if you need to detour to the main road for refreshments.

North-west across Tralee Bay to the tombolo

- Otherwise, continue straight on along the gorse-lined boreen, crossing six stiles beside gates in the next kilometre. The vegetation changes to tall holly and birch around the long-deserted hamlet of Killelton with its historic church. Then come three more stiles, two streams and a small gate, beyond which is a tarmac road (with main road access to the left).

- Follow the road and its earthen extension to a stile; descend on a wide, boggy boreen for 1·4 km to a sharp right bend. Then, it's up on a narrow path, cross a stile and continue climbing with good views over Derrymore 'Island'. A sign marks a turn-off to the N86, and this climb is nearly over.

- Shortly after the descent starts, swing right along the railway sleepers. Cross a bump and then drop down to Derrymore River bridge. The path then wanders up and down, crosses two stiles and soon passes a slender standing stone.

- The Way then diverges from its established line for a few hundred metres, climbing steeply to the right (south-east). Eventually you descend to cross Derryquay River. The path then bumps along, its surface sometimes rocky, sometimes grassy.

- A short climb takes you into the valley of Curraheen River, with Blennerville windmill serving as a landmark. Cross Curraheen River. (Shortly a track to the left gives access to the N86.)

- Gradually losing height, the Way crosses three small streams and passes the Tonavane Walk viewpoint, where you might see Brandon Mountain to the west. Descend through a gate to reach a tarmac road, and turn left.

Blennerville, with canal and windmill

- Follow this minor road south for 1·2 km to a T-junction; turn right and go on for nearly 1 km to another T-junction and turn left.

- After another 700 m you reach Blennerville, where you bear left to the N86. The Tralee & Blennerville Steam Railway used to run here: see panel.

- Cross the N86 and turn right along the footpath which leads to two bridges. Cross the road to pick up the canalside path.

- At the end of the canal (1·5 km along) turn right, to the N86. Go left and keep on the same side to the nearby roundabout, and turn left.

- Soon you reach James Street on the left. Cross the main road here and turn left to a gate on the right, which opens into The Green. Walk through to the gate, and the Dingle Way signboard is a few steps to the left on its far side.

The Tralee & Dingle Steam Railway was a famous narrow-gauge line, open from 1891-1953. Its 50 km track included some extreme gradients including a 1:30 stretch through Gleann na n'Gealt. After many accidents, it was closed, though some viaducts and bridges are still visible, and you walk on some of its sleepers when crossing boggy parts of the Dingle Way.

In 1993, the Tralee-Blennerville section was re-opened, its carriages hauled by an original Hunslet locomotive, the last surviving example, rescued in 1986. Trains used to run almost daily in season, but sadly the railway has not worked since 2006. Contact the Tralee Tourist Office for any updates: tel 353 66 712 1288.

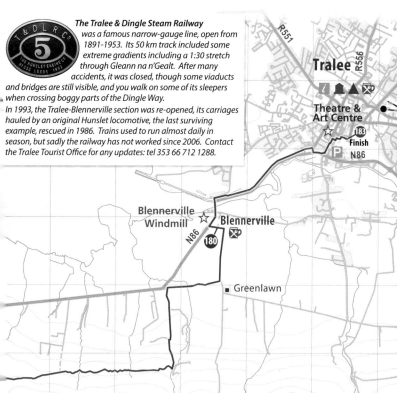

4 Reference

Further reading

Hendroff, Adrian *The Dingle Peninsula - A Walking Guide* 2015, Collins Press 128 pp, 978-1-8488-9233-0
Guide to 24 walks, most of which connect with or overlap the Dingle Way; useful for people who want to create circular routes.

Hayes-McCoy, F *Dingle and its Hinterland* 2017, Collins 224 pp, 978-1-848893-08-5
An insider guide to Dingle's history and heritage, supported by conversations with local people and many photographs.

Severin, Tim *The Brendan Voyage* 2005 Gill & Macmillan, 280 pp, 978-0-7171-3927-9
Compelling and adventurous account of the authentic recreation of St Brendan's 6th century boat and his likely route across the Atlantic.

Smith, Michael *An Unsung Hero: Tom Crean, Antarctic Survivor* 2009 Collins, 341 pp, 978-1-9051-7286-3
Readable biography of the modest, heroic Annascaul man who took part in three Antarctic expeditions (1901-1916).

Stagles, Ray and Redican, Sue *Blasket Island Guide* O'Brien Press 96 pp 2011 978-1-847172-16-7
Compact and informative booklet with colour photographs.

Maps

The Ordnance Survey Ireland Discovery Series (1:50,000) covers the Way with sheets 70 (5th ed 2015) and 71 (4th ed 2012). As of 2019, those were still current, but change is inevitable: always obtain the latest editions. Beware: OSi shows other waymarked walks using exactly the same pecked red line as the Dingle Way! OSi maps are available locally or direct from *www.irishmaps*.

Websites

A helpful website for readers of this book is the independent *www.dingleway.com*

The site *www.dingle-peninsula.ie* offers a visitor's guide to sights and attractions, with accommodation and other facilities in the towns and villages. It is more helpful than Kerry tourism sites that combine Dingle with its larger neighbour Iveragh. The Irish Tourist Board (Fáilte Ireland) has a website at *www.discoverireland.ie*. which lists accomodation, but it's selective: best searched by village name or map view. It has a section on the Wild Atlantic Way. The Irish Sports Council website has a section on National Waymarked Trails, with Dingle as number 11:
www.irishtrails.ie
Locally, Tralee Tourist Information Centre, in Ashe Memorial Hall (tel 353 66 712 1288) and Dingle Tourist Information Centre in Dingle town (tel 353 66 915 1188) are both open all year. (Within Ireland, from a landline omit the 353 and precede the number with 0.)

Hostels and camping

An Óige (Irish Youth Hostel Association) runs a hostel in Dublin but as of 2019 none on the Way. Happily several independent bodies run hostels: Independent Holiday Hostels of Ireland has one in Tralee: *www.hostels-ireland.com,* and two hostels in Annascaul are listed on *www.annascaul.ie.*
Hostel World lists several hostels at Dingle, and also ones at Annascaul and Inch: *www.hostelworld.com.*
Unique Irish Hostels lists four hostels on the Way, at Ballydavid, Cloghane, Dingle and Dunquin:
www.uniqueirishhostels.com
The Irish Caravan & Camping Council (*www.camping-ireland.ie*) publishes an annual guide with detailed campsite listings. In 2019, sites typically charge €15-20 for a small tent. There are designated campsites on or near the Way at Dingle and Castlegregory. Some hostels allow camping in their grounds; ask beforehand.

Transport

For information on how to get from anywhere to Tralee, we recommend the website *www.rome2rio.com.*

Flights to Dublin

Aer Lingus   *www.aerlingus.com*
British Airways   *www.ba.com*
Ryanair   *www.ryanair.com*

Over 40 other airlines fly direct to Dublin from all over the world. For transfers from the airport and buses within Dublin, refer to

Dublin Bus   *www.dublinbus.ie*

Flights from Dublin to Kerry

Aer Lingus   *www.aerlingus.com*

Flights direct to Kerry

Ryanair   *www.ryanair.com*
Kerry Airport   *www.kerryairport.ie*

Trains Dublin to Tralee

Iarnród Éireann   *www.irishrail.ie*
(Irish Rail)

Buses Dublin to Tralee

Bus Éireann   *www.buseireann.ie*

Ferries to Dublin from the UK

Irish Ferries   *www.irishferries.com*
Stena Line   *www.stenaline.com*

Guided and self-guided walks

Various options for Dingle Way holidays with baggage transfer and accommodation are offered by Wonderful Ireland:
www.walkingholiday.ie.

Other tour operators are listed on our website: please visit
www.rucsacs.com/books/dgw.

Weather forecast

Met Éireann (the Irish weather office) provides forecasts for up to 7 days ahead: visit *www.met.ie* and click on the map for Dingle.

Notes for novices

Our website offers advice on gear and preparation from the foot of our home page *www.rucsacs.com.*

Acknowledgements

We offer grateful thanks to Peter Galvin of Wonderful Ireland who generously shared many updates with us. This revised edition owes him a great debt, but any errors that remain are our responsibility. We thank also Eoin Reilly (*www.trailhead.ie*) and all those who commented on previous editions. Deepest thanks also to Lindsay Merriman for her careful proofreading.

Photo credits

Sandra Bardwell pp14-15, p24 (upper), p34 (both), p37, p68 (lower); **Mark Hamblin**/*rspb-images.com* p25 (lower); **Chris Knights**/*rspb-images.com* p23 (lower); **Gareth McCormack** front cover, p26, p38 (upper); **Peter Lenahan** via www.findagrave.com p66 (upper); **Jacquetta Megarry** title page, p4, p5, p6 (both), p7 (both), p8, p9, p11, p12, p17 (upper), p18 (both), p19, p20, p21 (all 3), p22, p23 (upper), p24 (lower), p25 (upper), p27 (both), p29, p30, p33 (inset), p36, p38 (lower), p43 (upper), pp46-7, p47 (upper), p48, p49 (upper), p50, p52, p53, pp54-5, p58, p59 (upper), pp60-61, p62, p65, p68-9, back cover; **Gordon Simm** p24 (middle) and p25 (middle). We thank *www.geograph.org.uk* for two images: Anne Patterson p54 (upper); Gareth James pp32-3. We thank also *Dreamstime.com* and photographers for these 12 images: Hel080808 p28; Richard Williams p35; Miroslav Liska p39; Thomas Marchhart p40; Daniel M. Cisilino p42 (upper) and pp16-17; Gunold pp42-3; Iryna Vlasenko p45; Stefano Valeri p49 (lower); Fotomorgana p57; Julia Middleton p59 (lower); Alisonbowden pp66-7.

Index